HEROES OF AMERICAN HISTORY

George Washington
The First President

Carin T. Ford

Enslow Publishers, Inc.

40 Industrial Road   PO Box 38
Box 398   Aldershot
Berkeley Heights, NJ 07922   Hants GU12 6BP
USA   UK

http://www.enslow.com

Library of Congress Cataloging-in-Publication Data

Ford, Carin T.
   George Washington—first president / Carin T. Ford.
     p. cm. — (Heroes of American history)
   Summary: A biography of the man who led the colonial army in its fight for independence from England and went on to become a new nation's first president.
   Includes index.
   ISBN 0-7660-1999-3
   1. Washington, George, 1732–1799—Juvenile literature. 2. Presidents—United States—Biography—Juvenile literature. [1. Washington, George, 1732–1799. 2. Presidents.] I. Title. II. Series.
   E312.66 .F67 2002
   973.4'1'092—dc21

                                       2002000491

Printed in the United States of America

10 9 8 7 6 5 4 3 2 1

To Our Readers: We have done our best to make sure all Internet Addresses in this book were active and appropriate when we went to press. However, the author and the publisher have no control over and assume no liability for the material available on those Internet sites or on other Web sites they may link to. Any comments or suggestions can be sent by e-mail to comments@enslow.com or to the address on the back cover.

Every effort has been made to locate all copyright holders of material used in this book. If any errors or omissions have occurred, corrections will be made in future editions of this book.

Table of Contents

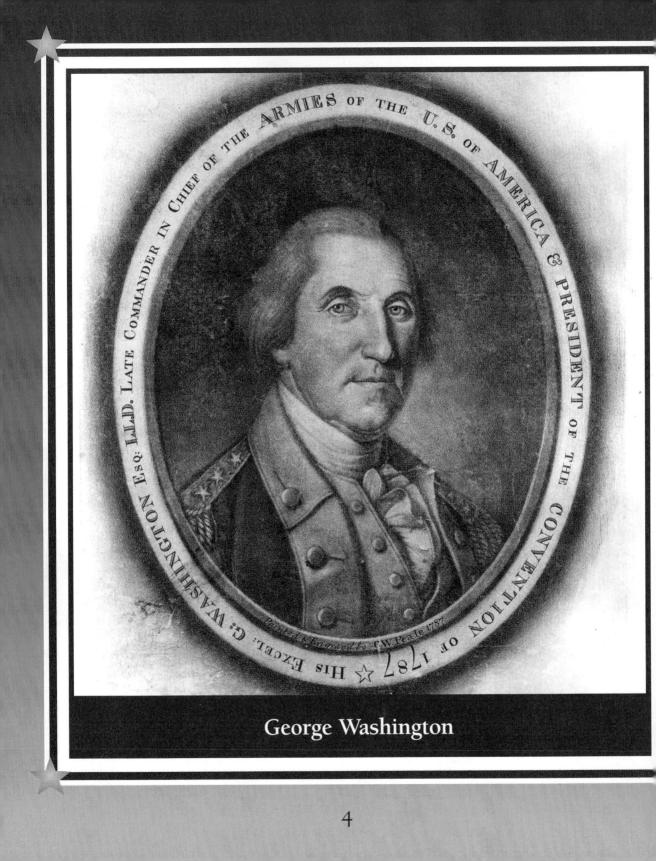

HIS EXCEL: G: WASHINGTON Esq: LLD. LATE COMMANDER IN CHIEF OF THE ARMIES OF THE U.S. OF AMERICA & PRESIDENT OF THE CONVENTION OF 1787

Painted & Engraved by C.W. Peale 1787

George Washington

Chapter 1

Early Learning

 oung George Washington liked to pretend he was fighting in battles. He used a cornstalk for a gun. George led his friends as they marched and fought.

When he grew up, George would lead a real army. He would guide the men of the American colonies in their fight for freedom from England.

George was born on February 22, 1732, in a farmhouse in Virginia. At that time, Virginia was

As a boy, George liked to pretend he was sword fighting with his friends.

one of thirteen American colonies owned by England. The colonists had to obey the laws set by the English king.

George was the oldest of six children born to Augustine and Mary Washington. George also had two older brothers and a sister from his father's first marriage. As a boy, George studied reading, writing, and arithmetic.

In school, George had to copy a list of 110 rules for good manners. One rule was that you should not clean your teeth with the tablecloth.

George's mother, Mary Washington.

George became an expert horseback rider and often followed his father around their tobacco farm. He was also interested in the tools his father used for surveying. This means measuring and mapping areas of land.

George's father planned to send him to school in England when he was older. But then his father died. George was only eleven, but his mother needed him to help run the family farm.

George started to spend more time with his older brother Lawrence. Lawrence served as an officer in Virginia's army, and George admired him very much.

George, below, learned about surveying land from his father.

At Lawrence's plantation, called Mount Vernon, George learned to hunt and fish. Lawrence also made sure his brother took lessons in fencing, which is fighting with a sword. He believed that George might be a good soldier one day.

George, center, helped his mother run the family farm and take care of the younger children.

Chapter 2

Fighting the French

eorge had always been interested in arithmetic. He also enjoyed surveying, just like his father. He practiced his skills by measuring a garden field, a pine forest, and other plots of land.

At age sixteen, George went on a surveying trip in Virginia. It was his first look at the American wilderness. Besides helping the surveyors, George learned about cooking out and camping under the stars.

When George was just seventeen, he was hired as the surveyor for Culpepper County, Virginia. For months at a time, he lived in the wilderness. There, he measured the land and drew maps. With the money he earned, George began buying some land of his own.

George helped the surveyors on his trip into the wilderness of Virginia.

George's brother Lawrence grew very sick. In 1751 the two brothers traveled to the island of Barbados in the West Indies. Lawrence hoped the warmer weather would make him better.

But the trip did not help Lawrence. Then George also became ill. He had caught smallpox, a disease

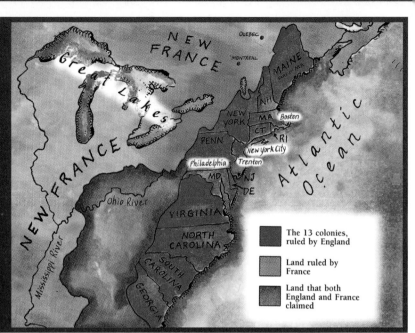

In the 1700s, when George was a young man, much of North America was owned by England and by France.

The 13 colonies, ruled by England

Land ruled by France

Land that both England and France claimed

that can be deadly. Luckily, George got well, though his face was left with some scars. Lawrence died in 1752, and twenty-year-old George became the owner of Mount Vernon.

In those days, England ruled all the American colonies. But France also claimed that it had rights to land in America, especially in the Ohio River Valley. England and France often fought each other to see who would control this land.

When he was in his early twenties, George was asked to help drive the French out of this area. The struggle became known as the French and Indian War. Many American Indians fought on the side of the French. Others fought alongside the English.

George wrote that there was "sharp firing on both sides. . . . I heard the bullets whistle."

The battles raged for several years, and George was in the middle of the action. Twice, the horse he was riding was shot out from under him. Another time, bullets tore through his clothing. George became known for his bravery on the battlefield.

After five years, George was ready to leave the army.

George, on horseback, was a brave soldier in the French and Indian War.

The war was not over, and all the officers of his company begged George not to go.

But George, now twenty-six, had fallen in love with Martha Custis. She was a widow with two small children, Jackie and Patsy. George and Martha were married on January 6, 1759. George looked forward to taking care of his family and farms. He also wanted to serve in Virginia's government, which was called the House of Burgesses.

George was ready to start a new life.

George married Martha Custis in 1759.

Chapter 3

Army Leader

For the next sixteen years, George lived the life of a wealthy southern planter. It was a hard job, and there were many things George had to take care of. He awoke before the sun came up, hopped on his horse, and rode about his huge plantation.

Mount Vernon was more like a town than a farm. Fish and pigs were raised on the farm, along with wheat, corn, and other fruits and vegetables.

Blacksmiths made axes and plows and fitted horses with shoes. Carpenters put up new buildings. Tailors and shoemakers stitched clothing for George's family and the hundreds of slaves on the farm.

George liked running Mount Vernon, and he could have spent the rest of his life there. But he knew that the colonies were having troubles with England. The English king wanted the people in the colonies to help pay for the French and Indian War. England began placing heavy taxes on goods such as sugar, paper, and tea.

Mount Vernon was more like a town than a farm.

George had many slaves at Mount Vernon. They worked in the fields and in the house.

The colonists were angry. Why should they pay taxes to England when they had no say in the English government?

The English government wanted to calm down the colonists, so it removed most of the taxes. Only the tax on tea remained.

Still, the colonists thought this was unfair. When they complained, England sent soldiers to force the colonists to obey.

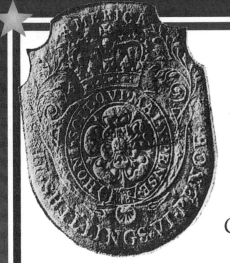

By the fall of 1774, a group of American leaders met to talk about the future of the colonies. George attended this first meeting of the Continental Congress in Philadelphia, Pennsylvania.

The colonists were told to pay taxes on all paper goods printed with this tax stamp. This English law made them very angry.

In April 1775, fighting broke out between the English soldiers and the colonists. Many people started saying that the American colonies should break away from England's rule. They wanted America to be its own, independent country.

At the next meeting of the Continental Congress, in May 1775, George was elected to run the colonists' new army. He would lead the Americans in their fight for freedom from England.

George set out on horseback for Boston, ready to

take command. He was shocked that his army was made up of 14,000 ordinary men—just farmers, shopkeepers, and fishermen. They were not trained as soldiers. George had a lot of work ahead of him.

George's army needed supplies, such as guns, bullets, food, medicine, and blankets.

By March 1776, George and his soldiers had driven the English army out of Boston. He was called a hero.

But the war was just beginning. There were many years of fighting still to come.

The Continental Congress chose George to lead the army against England.

General Washington trained his men to be soldiers.

Chapter 4

Victory
for America

Four months after the English fled from Boston, the Declaration of Independence was written. In this important paper, the colonists stated that America was a free country, no longer under England's rule.

George and his men went to New York City. There, he bravely led his troops into battle. "I will fight as long as I have a leg or an arm," he said.

The Americans were not able to defeat the

English in New York. George did not have enough men or supplies. Also, diseases such as typhoid fever and smallpox swept through the army. Thousands of soldiers became sick, and many died.

George and his men crossed the icy Delaware River to surprise the English in the Battle of Trenton.

The Americans had some success in Trenton, New Jersey, in 1776. On Christmas night, George caught the English soldiers by surprise. George and his army captured the city.

George saw his men through

George led his men to victory in the Battle of Yorktown.

many rough times, including a hard winter in Valley Forge, Pennsylvania. The soldiers had little food or clothing. Men without boots marched barefoot through snow and ice.

The Revolutionary War was long and bloody. In 1778, France decided to help the Americans. The French sent soldiers and money to the colonies.

In October 1781, George won an important battle in Yorktown, Virginia. The English army surrendered.

During the Revolutionary War, George was a brave, strong leader.

Finally, the fighting was over. Peace talks began the next year. By 1783, the Thirteen Colonies were a separate country, called the United States of America.

George was now almost fifty years old. He was ready to go home to Mount Vernon. He wanted to work on his farm and lead a quiet life.

But someone was needed to be the leader of the new country. Again, everyone looked to George.

Chapter 5

First President

According to the country's new set of laws—called the U.S. Constitution—Americans would vote to choose their president. This was different from other countries, where the people had no say in choosing their kings and queens.

George did not want to be president. But once again, his country needed him. So, at the age of fifty-seven, George became the first president of the

New-York

Inauguration of Washington

United States. He took office on April 30, 1789, in New York City, the capital at that time. A year later, the capital was moved to Philadelphia.

As the first president, George had many decisions to make. He needed to organize the government. He had to help the United States get along with American Indians and with other countries.

George handled these problems with great skill. He made peace with the American Indians. He kept the United States out of a war in Europe by signing treaties with England and Spain. He also helped choose the location for a new capital city to be built along the Potomac River. It would be called Washington, in his honor.

In 1792, George was elected to serve for another four years as president. During these years, three more states joined the new nation: Kentucky, Tennessee, and Vermont.

After George's second term as the president, the people still wanted him as their leader. But George did not want to run for a third time. He finally went home to Mount Vernon in 1797.

Being president was a very hard job.

For the next two and a half years, George enjoyed his life at Mount Vernon. Then one day, after riding around the farm on his horse, George caught a cold.

George Washington died in 1799 with his wife, Martha, at his side.

He soon became very sick, and he died on December 14, 1799. He was sixty-seven years old.

George Washington was one of America's most beloved leaders. He played a key role in the country's fight for freedom. He helped shape the new nation and is remembered as the "Father of Our Country."

Timeline

1732~Born on February 22.

1748~Takes a job as a surveyor in Virginia.

1754~Leads a unit of British soldiers
      against the French.

1759~Marries Martha Custis.

1775~Is named commander in chief of
      the Continental Army.

1781~Defeats the English soldiers at Yorktown.

1789~Is elected first president of the United States.

1791~Helps select the land that will become the
      nation's new capital, Washington, D.C.

1797~Retires after two terms as
      president.

1799~Dies at home in Mount Vernon
      on December 14.

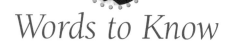

Words to Know

Continental Congress—A meeting of American leaders to discuss the future of the colonies.

Declaration of Independence—The historic paper in which the American colonies state their freedom from England.

French and Indian War—A war from 1754 to 1763 in which France and England fought for control of the Ohio River Valley.

plantation—A very large farm.

Revolutionary War—A war from 1775 to 1783 in which the thirteen American colonies fought for freedom from England's rule.

surveyor—A person who measures land to find out its boundaries.

U.S. Constitution—The laws for the new government of the United States.

Learn More

Books

Fritz, Jean. *George Washington's Breakfast.*
New York: Paper Star, 1998.

Giblin, James Cross. *George Washington: A Picture Book Biography.* New York: Scholastic Trade, 1998.

Heilbroner, Joan and Marchesi, Stephen. *Meet George Washington.* New York: Random House, 2001.

Internet Addresses

A short biography and some links to more information.
<http://www.americaslibrary.gov/cgi-bin/page.cgi/aa/wash>

A variety of information and links.
<http://www.ipl.org/div/potus/gwashington.html>

Index